Medieval Tiles: A Handbook

Medieval Tiles

E. S. EAMES

PUBLISHED FOR
THE TRUSTEES OF THE BRITISH MUSEUM
BY
BRITISH MUSEUM PUBLICATIONS LIMITED

© *1968, The Trustees of the British Museum*

ISBN O 7141 1326 3 paper
ISBN O 7141 1337 9 cased

First published 1968
Reprinted 1976

Published by British Museum Publications Ltd.
6 Bedford Square, London WC1B 3RA

Printed in Great Britain
Plates printed by George Over Limited Rugby and London
Text printed at the University Press, Oxford

Contents

List of Plates

All of the tiles illustrated are in the collections of the Department of British and Medieval Antiquities, British Museum

Acknowledgements

I am indebted to the following for the use of information that is not yet fully published: the late Professor H. Swinnerton, Lenton kilns; Mr Stuart Rigold, East Kent industry; Mr Robert Thompson, Nuneaton kilns; Mr Laurence Keen and Mr John Malden, Llanthony Priory at Gloucester and sixteenth-century West Country inlaid tile industry.

I should also like to thank Mr G. K. Beaulah for permission to publish his reconstruction of the Meaux kiln, and to acknowledge permission from Her Majesty's Stationery Office to reproduce the Byland pavement plan.

Introduction

The British Museum has an unrivalled collection of decorated English medieval tiles. It contains a few wall tiles but the rest are floor tiles and these include one complete pavement and several large pieces of paving. The tiles range in date from the second quarter of the thirteenth century to the middle of the sixteenth century and are decorated in several techniques. It is probable that none of these techniques originated in England, but the continental origins and affinities have not yet been fully worked out.

Some decorated floor tiles seem to have been used in England before the thirteenth century, a few even before the Norman Conquest, but, as far as is known at present, these appear as occasional isolated instances of the use of decorated tiles for paving, and it was not until the second quarter of the thirteenth century that tiled pavements began to be used regularly in steadily increasing numbers. One may regard tiled floors, along with glazed windows, wall chimneys and internal stairs, as part of the trend towards comfort observable in royal residences and the wealthier ecclesiastical buildings during the thirteenth century and passing into more general use in middle class buildings during the fourteenth century. Decorated English floor tiles continued to be readily available during the fourteenth and fifteenth centuries, but during the earlier part of the sixteenth century the English industry was killed by the changes in fashion attendant upon the Renaissance. Native techniques continued to be employed only in the west country where some tiles decorated in the medieval manner are known to have been made in Barnstaple as late as the eighteenth century.

Several different techniques were used to provide the decoration, but all have one thing in common: they depend upon body clays and glazes for their colours, no paints or enamels being used. Moreover the production of a polychrome tile by the use of different coloured glazes is so rare in the period under discussion that it cannot be included as a regular technique. A polychrome effect in a pavement was obtained by the use of different coloured tiles, and a polychrome pattern on a tile was obtained by the use of different coloured body clays. The most usual way of obtaining this was by inlaying a design in white-firing clay into the red earthenware body. This method produced the tiles which most nineteenth-century writers called 'encaustic', an unfortunate choice of term because no enamels were used.

The glazes were all lead glazes such as were used on contemporary pottery. Five colours could be obtained in the following way: brown by applying a lead glaze direct to a red earthenware body; yellow by applying a lead glaze over an inlay or slip coating of white-firing clay; light green by applying lead glaze with an addition of copper over a white slip; dark green by applying the same glaze direct to the red earthenware body; near black by applying the lead glaze with a higher proportion of copper direct to the earthenware body. A purplish black was sometimes produced when the minerals in the glaze contained manganese but its presence is thought to have been accidental, and much the same effect was sometimes caused by over firing. Most of the near black glazes that have been analysed have proved to contain only a higher proportion of copper.

The green glaze was too opaque to be used successfully on tiles which depended for their decoration on different coloured body clays, although a few tiles on which this had been attempted are known. The inlaid tiles were glazed with the clear lead glaze. When this was fired it appeared brown over the red body and yellow over the white inlay. This produced the characteristic brown tile with a yellow pattern on it, so widely reproduced in the nineteenth century and so favoured by the church restorers of that period.

These nineteenth-century reproductions copy the medieval designs with meticulous accuracy, but they can never be mistaken for medieval tiles. The clays and glazes from which they were manufactured were scientifically mixed, and fired in controlled conditions, which produced a close body of uniform colour and texture covered with a uniform glaze. The designs were impressed with plaster dies, which gave clear cut edges, and they stand out sharply yellow. As a result whole pavements were produced which contained no variations of colour or texture and the effect tended to be staring and unpleasing. On the other hand no two medieval tiles ever turned out exactly alike. The body clays were mixed by rule of thumb, sometimes surprisingly carelessly. The glazes were rarely distributed evenly and the copper content of the green glaze was never evenly absorbed; moreover the texture of the tile was coarse and its surface slightly uneven so that concentrations of glaze gathered in little depressions with a resulting deepening of colour.

Further variation was caused by inequalities of firing. Over-fired tiles may appear near purple with irridescent and lustrous patches. Large numbers, particularly of the earlier tiles, have a reduced grey core where oxygen failed to penetrate during the last stage of firing. When, as frequently happened, these grey patches reached the surface they completely altered the appearance of the glaze to a dull olive green. The presence of these unoxidised patches at or near the surface may be due in part to the fact that the English tiles were glazed before they were fired. When the glaze had formed a coating over the surface it may have hindered the penetration of oxygen into the tile through that side.

Contemporary Dutch and Flemish tiles seem to have been biscuit fired and then glazed and fired again. All of the evidence found so far in England demonstrates that here the tiles were fired once only, having been glazed while still green. The continental method produced a glassier surface which seems sometimes to have chipped or flaked in wear. The English method did not produce quite such a high gloss but does seem to have produced an area of fusion between the glaze and the body so that the glaze seems not to have flaked but just to have worn through gradually, with the result that the English tiles often retain the lower levels, and therefore the colour, of the glaze after the gloss of the surface has worn away.

Tile Mosaic

PLAIN MOSAIC

Apart from the isolated occurrences of decorated tile paving that are known before the thirteenth century, the earliest tile pavements in England that can be reasonably securely dated were made of two-colour ceramic mosaic. The colours used were dark green and yellow and these are thought to be the nearest that could be obtained to the black and white marble of contemporary Italian floors. Shaped components of alternate colours were used to build up the patterns, so that the finished mosaic depended for its effect both on the shape of the individual tiles and on the alternation of the two colours, although each tile was of one colour only. Many of the patterns resemble Italian examples. Most are fairly simple geometric forms, but elaborate shapes of birds, fleurs de lys and Gothic tracery were also used.

The area to be paved was divided into panels marked out by strips of rectilinear tiles, usually squares or oblong and triangular halves of squares. Each panel was then paved with tiles forming one mosaic pattern. The panels were generally laid out fairly symmetrically on the floor, but there was considerable freedom in the arrangement of patterns within that framework. Plate XIII shows the layout of a tile mosaic pavement still *in situ* in the south transept of the church at Byland Abbey. The British Museum possesses about half of a panel corresponding to the large circular panel on the plan and smaller sections from Byland, Meaux and Rievaulx Abbeys. Colour plate A shows one of these pieces from Rievaulx and the cover picture shows another. One corresponds to a pattern from Byland shown on the plan at Plate XIII. These pieces of tile mosaic were not found *in situ* but were reassembled from loose tiles recovered from the various abbey sites.

Although most of the tile mosaic known in England comes from Cistercian Abbeys, the earliest piece to which a date can be assigned with reasonable certainty is in Canterbury cathedral, which was Benedictine. This is a very small portion of pavement in the extreme east end of the corona of Saint Thomas, where it was probably laid in about 1220. Tile mosaic of exactly the same

A. A section of tile mosaic from the Cistercian Abbey at Rievaulx, Yorkshire. Rutland Collection, Rievaulx cabinet.

B. A restored roundel depicting King Richard I in combat with Saladin, within a restored frame of four tiles making a 16-inch square; all from the site of Chertsey Abbey, Surrey. Collection of Chertsey tiles.

type as that used in the English Cistercian houses has been found on the sites of continental Cistercian houses as well, and it is not known whether the technique originated in England or abroad. It is, however, fairly certain that all of the tile mosaic known in

Fig. 1. Reconstruction of a mid-thirteen-century kiln for firing tile mosaic based on remains excavated at North Grange, Meaux, near Beverley, Yorkshire, drawn by G. K. Beaulah, Esq.

England was made in this country, probably at or very close to the place where it was used. Although the same patterns are repeated at various sites, the differences in the body fabric of tiles of the same shape from different sites exclude the possibility that there was a single place of manufacture. However, the site of only one kiln producing tile mosaic has been found so far. This is at North Grange, Meaux, near Beverley in Yorkshire, and it was used to fire the mosaic tiles used in the church at Meaux Abbey. Sufficient waste tile and structural debris was recovered for the main features of the kiln and the methods of manufacture of the tiles to be ascertained. A selection of this material is in the British Museum. The Abbey church at Meaux was paved between 1249 and 1269 and may have been one of the last places to have a plain tile mosaic floor. A drawing showing the probable form of the kiln is reproduced as figure 1.

DECORATED MOSAIC

Two elaborations of this plain tile mosaic were developed. In the simpler of these, patterns were impressed on the surface of some of the mosaic shapes, either in fairly solid intaglio or in linear outline. The former type occurs at Meaux Abbey and the latter at Coggeshall Abbey and Prior Crauden's Chapel, Ely and various other East Anglian and East Midland sites. Two pieces from Meaux Abbey, one a simple square, are illustrated Plate 1 : 1 and 2, and Plate 1 : 3 shows a mosaic cinquefoil decorated with six linear cinquefoils from Pipewell Abbey, Northamptonshire. The depressions made in the surface of the tiles were left empty and each tile continued to be of one colour.

In the more elaborate technique, designs impressed in the surface of the mosaic shapes were inlaid with white-firing clay with the result that each tile so treated was of two colours, brown and yellow. As has been mentioned, inlaying could not be combined successfully with green glazes and therefore decorated brown and yellow shapes had to be used with plain dark green shapes. The result was that the decorated brown and yellow tiles were given pride of place in the layout of the pavement and the dark tiles were relegated to the function of providing contrasting bands to separate one patterned section from another. Paving of this type is therefore not a true mosaic of alternating colours, but it is a form of mosaic because the shapes of the tiles, as well as their decoration, contribute to the pattern. It may for convenience be called inlaid mosaic. This technique was most frequently used for great circular patterns composed of concentric bands of brown and yellow inlaid tiles separated by narrow bands of plain dark green tiles. A segment of a great circular pattern of this type is illustrated on Plate II. This dates from about 1244 and was part of the pavement of the King's private chapel at Clarendon Palace near Salisbury. The chapel had been on an upper floor, which had collapsed long before the tiles were recovered from the ruins of the building during excavations in the 1930's. These tiles have now been re-assembled in the British Museum. The kiln in which they were fired was discovered in 1937. Plate xv shows a photograph of the remains *in situ* in 1965 immediately before they were removed to the British Museum. Plate xvi shows a model made in 1939 to demonstrate the form of the arches which had carried the oven floor. Other great circular patterns of this type have been found at a number of sites, but inlaid tile mosaic in its most elaborate form and highest degree of artistic and technical excellence has been recovered from the site of Chertsey Abbey in Surrey.

CHERTSEY INLAID TILE MOSAIC

The thirteenth-century inlaid tiles from Chertsey Abbey are justly the most famous decorated medieval tiles in England. The museum possesses the greatest number of those known, running into many hundreds of tiles and fragments, and including most of those rescued from the site by Dr Manwaring Shurlock and published by him in 1885. The reputation of these tiles rests on a series of large roundels between 9 and 10 inches in diameter, decorated with pictorial subjects drawn by a first class artist and translated into the medium of inlaid tile with a degree of technical skill never again achieved.

Thirty-four identified pictures illustrate the romance of Tristram and Isolde and there are a number of fragments from other pictures in the same series, too small to be reconstructed or identified. It is possible that the pictorial roundels were designed for the tiles, but it is more probable that the tile dies were copied from existing decorative roundels illustrating a manuscript of the romance of Tristram and Isolde, although no manuscript with comparable pictures is known to survive.

Nine other pictorial roundels are for convenience referred to as the Richard Coeur de Lion series. Two of these certainly represent the slaying of Saladin by Richard in single combat. That depicting King Richard is illustrated on Colour Plate B. A third may show Richard fighting the lion in the incident from which he derived his name, but the rest show various forms of single combat, either between a man and a lion or between two men. The combat may be the linking theme of this group of pictures. Again it is possible that they are based on manuscript illustrations. The story of Richard I's prowess was a favourite one with his nephew Henry III, who is known to have used it as the decorative theme in several rooms in various royal dwellings. In general the treatment of the figures in this series is more fluid than that in the Tristram series, but the designs may be by the same hand.

These great roundels were combined with various other sets of tiles in the pavements, and as none of these was found *in situ* it is not possible to say whether both series of pictures were used with all the different surrounds, or whether some surrounds belong to the Richard pictures and some to the Tristram pictures. Plate III shows an assemblage devised by Dr Shurlock and published by Henry Shaw in 1858. Many of the circular bands surrounding the pictures, shown here as circles of decorative crowns, contained inscriptions relating the story depicted. Most of the letters which made up these inscriptions were inlaid singly on small segmental tiles, but fortunately some were inlaid in groups, mainly of three letters, on longer tiles. Some of these bear the words: REX, LEO and RICA, confirming the identification of some of the pictures and demonstrating that the inscriptions referring to the Richard series were in Latin. Others bear the names: MARC, MORGAN, MORHAUT and a contraction of Tristram. The parts of other words which are with them show that the inscriptions belonging to the Tristram series were in Norman French.

The foliate scrolls which decorate the surrounding mosaic exist in three distinct forms of which this is the most elaborate. In another, probably later, form the mosaic element in the surrounds was discarded, and the roundels were enclosed in a frame of four large tiles which together made up a 16-inch square. Both a quarter of the foliate scroll work and a quarter of the circular band were included on each tile. This type of surround is shown on Colour Plate B where the circular band is decorated with a pair of grotesques. In the last phase the Tristram pictures were reproduced on rectangular tiles about 9 inches square, flanked by architectural borders. In this form they were probably used in conjunction with an elaborate series of panels depicting a king, a queen, an archbishop and a crucifixion under architectural canopies.

Tiles of this series of panels and of the Tristram pictures on square tiles were found in the remains of a kiln discovered on the site of Chertsey Abbey in 1922 and thought to date from the earlier 1290's. The date of the first use of the pictorial roundels is not firmly fixed. Attempts have been made to date them on the form of the armour but this is naturally somewhat tentative, especially if one accepts the theory that existing manuscript illustrations were used as a basis for the pictures on the tiles. Until more is known, any date between 1250 and 1290 would seem acceptable and it is possible that the development of the series lasted throughout that time, the mosaic element becoming progressively simpler until by the 1290's it was abandoned altogether. Inlaid mosaic was used at Chertsey Abbey in other forms besides those associated with the great pictorial roundels and Plate IV: 1 shows a small assemblage, seven inches square, now in the British Museum.

Pictorial roundels of the Tristram series, identical to those used at Chertsey or closely related to them, were used at Hailes Abbey in Gloucestershire and at Halesowen Abbey in Worcestershire. At Halesowen additional pictorial tiles were made depicting monks and abbots. The most important of these is the seated figure of the Abbot Nicholas surrounded by an inscription stating that he had given the pavement. The inscription is incorporated in four large tiles designed to frame the roundels in the same way as the 4-tile 16-inch square frame used at Chertsey illustrated on Colour Plate B. Abbot Nicholas died in 1298/9, which is therefore the latest possible date for the commissioning of the pavement. Some of the pictorial tiles at Halesowen are rectangular and it can be deduced that here, as at Chertsey, the mosaic element was abandoned towards the end of the thirteenth century.

The reasons for discontinuing the manufacture of tile mosaic were almost certainly the extra labour and expense involved in the production of irregularly shaped tiles when compared with the production of square ones. Square tiles could be shaped rapidly in one or two standard sizes as a routine job, and when they were ready they were stacked on edge in rows in the oven in a series of criss cross tiers which required no special arrangement or kiln furniture. The mosaic shapes had to be drawn individually on a clay slab and then cut out. Simple rectilinear shapes were fired in rectangular blocks and broken apart afterwards, but complicated rectilinear shapes and all curvilinear shapes were cut out individually before they were glazed and fired. Stacks of these irregularly shaped pieces had to be carefully built and could not be carried up to the full height of the oven with the result that removable intermediate shelving had to be used. The drawing on figure 1 shows how this was probably arranged. This made the loading and unloading of the oven comparatively slow and complicated. When the mosaic tiles were laid the paviour had to place his intricate patterns accurately on the floor. Every process required time and skill and mosaic therefore did not lend itself to inexpensive mass production and was rarely made after the end of the thirteenth century.

Inlaid and Printed Tiles

EARLY INLAID TILES

The method of decorating tiles by stamping a pattern on the surface and filling the resulting depressions with a white-firing clay has already been described in connection with inlaid mosaic. It was introduced into this country as a fully developed technique, probably from Normandy, at least as early as the 1230's and possibly earlier. It was usually employed on a square red earthenware quarry. Tiles of this type were made in the same kiln as those for the great circular pavement in the King's chapel at Clarendon Palace, probably between 1237 and 1244. This is the kiln illustrated on Plates xv and xvi. There is documentary evidence for another active period of tile paving there from 1250 to 1253, and yet another in 1260. New kilns were set up, but so far only a waste heap from the kiln working in the 1250's has been located. The British Museum has a representative collection of these inlaid tiles from Clarendon Palace, including a complete portion of pavement from one of the Queen's chambers, made between 1250 and 1252. This is illustrated on Plate v. It shows the way in which it was usual to divide the floor into a number of panels. In this case the panels ran across the width of the room. The treatment of each panel is different and demonstrates the wide variety of effect that could be obtained by different combinations of plain and decorated tiles. Only six different inlaid designs are used in this piece of pavement.

Inlaid tile paving of this type rapidly became very popular and was produced in far greater quantity than any form of tile mosaic. The site of Chertsey Abbey has yielded a great variety of square inlaid tiles which appear to be contemporary with the inlaid mosaic and therefore probably date from the latter half of the thirteenth century. One tile showing a griffin in a circle is illustrated on Plate IV : 3. The original pavement of inlaid tiles can still be seen in Henry III's great octagonal chapter house at Westminster, completed in 1259. One tile from it is illustrated on Plate IV : 2. There is documentary evidence for the use of tile paving in the Palace of Westminster at this period, but none of this is known to survive. It is tempting to believe that two intrusive strips of pictorial tiles and inscriptions that break the continuity of the panels in the pavement of Westminster chapter house, were laid with tiles left over from a pictorial pavement in the palace. Tile paving was being carried out at a number of other royal residences in the middle decades of the thirteenth century, and of these Winchester castle was probably the most important for the future development of the decorated tile industry. The present evidence suggests that inlaid tile paving was introduced into England in the royal buildings of Henry III.

Technically these early inlaid tiles are good and sometimes excellent. The body fabric is fairly well mixed and well fired. The tiles are generally between 5 and 6 inches square, and about 1 inch thick. They usually have roughly circular depressions scooped out of the back. These probably hastened the drying of the tiles and acted as a keying into the mortar bed on which they were laid. The designs are well drawn and often intricate. They were impressed sharply into the tiles and have clean edges. The depth of the impression, and consequently of the inlay, varies, but it averages around one-tenth of an inch. The finished products convey the impression that every stage, from the designing and block making to the final laying of the tile, was carried out by competent and careful craftsmen who had all the time and resources that they needed to do the job properly.

THE WESSEX SCHOOL

The use of inlaid tile paving in royal buildings was followed immediately by the use of similar paving in neighbouring ecclesiastical buildings, probably while the tilers were still under royal patronage, and from there it spread out into a wider field. At Westminster, as has already been mentioned, the use of tile paving in the palace was followed by the paving of the chapter house, and that in its turn was followed by the paving of St Dunstan's chapel, which was not a royal building.

The great new cathedral church at Salisbury, dedicated in 1258, was paved with tiles inlaid with the same designs as those used at Clarendon Palace in the early 1250's, but it is interesting to notice that the body fabric of the tiles from the two places is not the same. This suggests that the cathedral tiles were not made in one of the palace kilns but at some other site probably in or near the Cathedral Close. The building of an octagonal chapter house followed the completion of the church. This too was paved with inlaid tiles arranged in an elaborate series of panels running in towards the centre of the floor. The present pavement is a nineteenth-century replica. A few of the tiles from the original are in the British Museum. Henry Shaw published drawings of the original pavement in 1858. It is interesting to notice that in this great pavement only six different square inlaid patterns are used, and of these, four are the same designs as four of the six used in the Queen's chamber at Clarendon, with very minor variations of detail. An additional decorative element was introduced in the chapter house by the use of some inlaid oblong and small square tiles. The tiles of these sizes in the Queen's chamber were plain. Somewhat later, possibly in the 1280's, an octagonal treasury and muniment room was built, and the muniment room at least was paved with inlaid tiles in an elaborate arrangement of panels comparable to that in the chapter house. The tiles are smaller and new blocks must therefore have been made to impress the patterns on them, but these were all adaptations of cathedral and chapter house designs.

From the cathedral the use of inlaid tiles spread to other buildings in Salisbury and thence into the surrounding districts. There are minor differences of size, design and fabric, but the general repertory of patterns and the manufacturing techniques remain the same. The conclusion to be drawn from this is that craftsmen moved from site to site, taking their blocks and patterns with them, but setting up their workshops and kilns near the place where the tiles were to be laid and using the local clays. It is interesting to notice that the simpler designs were those which were most frequently reproduced, but that as time went on these tended to be elaborated often detrimentally.

For want of a better term, the tile industry of this area is referred to as the Clarendon-Salisbury branch of the Wessex school. Its products are spread over Wiltshire and Somerset and some adjoining areas. It persisted through the fourteenth century and into the earlier part of the fifteenth. Tiles of this type were bought for Winchester College in 1412 at Newbury. There is at present no evidence that any factory site was established in this area and the products of the Midland and Chiltern factories did not reach it.

Very much the same sequence of events seems to have taken place in the Hampshire area, where the techniques employed and the organisation and development of the inlaid tile industry seem to have followed the same course as in the Clarendon-Salisbury area, but the series of decorative patterns employed is mainly different. These are derived from designs used at Westminster and Chertsey, which probably reached Hampshire through Winchester. Few of the tiles used in Winchester castle survive but it may be assumed that the tiles in the cathedral were derived from them and were substantially the same. There is no evidence that the Chertsey pictorial roundels were reused in this region, but pieces of the later Chertsey figure tile, depicting an archbishop, have been found at Winchester cathedral and at Preston Candover and it is possible that other tiles of that series were also used in the Winchester area. The patterns in this area tend to be more elaborate than those of the Clarendon-Salisbury series. The Westminster-Chertsey branch of the Wessex school was destined to have a wide distribution and influence north of the Thames.

THE MIDLAND FACTORY INDUSTRIES

The fourteenth century saw the rise of two major commercial inlaid tile industries in the Midlands, both derived from the thirteenth-century Westminster-Chertsey branch of the Wessex school. One was in Warwickshire, where Coventry and Nuneaton are known to have been centres, and the other was in Nottingham. It seems likely that inlaid tiles reached Warwickshire, as they had reached Wiltshire, as a result of a few special commissions executed in this region towards the close of the thirteenth century. Two abbeys used Chertsey designs including pictorial roundels: Hailes in Gloucestershire, and Halesowen in Worcestershire. At Hailes a very beautiful design, of which the main element is a branch of naturalistic oak leaves with acorns, retains a small corner element with Chertsey type stiff-leaved terminals. This is shown on Plate IV : 4. At Halesowen some new pictorial roundels were used depicting the abbots of the house as has been mentioned on page 9, above. Most important of these is the one showing Abbot Nicholas who died in 1298/9. This was surrounded by an inscription stating that Abbot Nicholas gave the work, presumably the pavement, to the Mother of Christ. This inscription is incorporated in four large tiles designed to frame the roundel. The remainder of these tiles outside the inscription is decorated with the same scroll work as that used at Chertsey and illustrated on Colour Plate B, but with naturalistic leaves replacing the stiff-leaved terminals. This pavement must have been designed, even if it was not completed, before the death of Abbot Nicholas in 1298/9. At Halesowen, Tristram pictures were also used on square tiles as in the last phase at Chertsey and other square tiles of the same size were decorated with new and cruder figures of seated abbots and standing monks. One of these is illustrated on Plate IV : 5. The British Museum has a very good collection of tiles from both sites.

In Warwickshire, tiles with both Chertsey and Hailes type foliate scroll designs have been found at Kenilworth Abbey and Maxstoke Priory, and Kenilworth has some tiles with well drawn figures of animals and grotesques, but neither site has yielded any of the Chertsey pictorial designs. Fragments of the Halesowen inscribed frame tile have been found in Coventry and it was thought that they came originally from the site of the

Priory there. Even more important, in 1911 the remains of a large kiln were found during building on Harefield estate, Stoke, Coventry, where many tiles, both perfect ones and wasters, are said to have been found in and around the kiln.

These were not published at the time, but fortunately in 1940 Mr Philip Chatwin published two photographs of the kiln and two figures of tile designs found on the kiln site. Among these is a rampant lion identical with one used at Halesowen. Chatwin's other figure of tiles from the Stoke kiln shows fragments of an otherwise unknown inlaid mosaic. The available information therefore suggests that expert tilers went to Hailes, Halesowen and Kenilworth Abbeys and perhaps to Coventry Priory towards the end of the thirteenth century to execute special commissions for elaborate tile pavements, which included inlaid mosaic, pictorial tiles, inscriptions and many other intricate designs. Some of them established a tilery at Stoke, Coventry, where suitable brick earth and the much rarer white-firing clay for the inlay were both available, and there they continued to manufacture inlaid tiles for other customers, discontinuing the more expensive features such as mosaic and pictorial inlay, and reproducing the simpler designs on standard rectangular quarries.

During the course of the fourteenth century, designs were modified and new ones were added. Large designs derived from Chertsey type foliate scrolls were devised to be made up from four, nine or sixteen square quarries, and many forms of naturalistic foliage were used. Heraldic shields became very popular. These were doubtless designed for particular customers, but once the blocks had been made the tile makers continued to use them and to sell tiles so decorated to customers who had no connection with the arms portrayed.

The later limits of the Stoke industry have not been defined, but the time range of the few patterns recorded from the site suggests that it persisted until the late fifteenth century. It is not known whether it was continuously active and it must not be imagined that the one kiln found was operating during the whole of the period, but it may be supposed that a series of kilns had occupied the same area. It is most unfortunate that no complete record of the tiles found there was published at the time. The general run of the Coventry factory tiles is not well represented in the British

Museum, but there is a large collection from the site of Maxstoke Priory. In 1967 a series of medieval pottery kilns covering a wide time range was excavated at Nuneaton, Warwickshire. In one of these, tile wasters of a type used at Halesowen Abbey were found associated with thirteenth-century pottery. There were no pictorial or mosaic pieces. As well as the pottery kilns one tile kiln was excavated. It yielded fourteenth-century inlaid tiles of a type known at a number of sites mainly in Leicestershire and adjoining counties. The British Museum has a number of tiles of this type from Ulverscroft Priory, Leicestershire.

The Nottingham industry does not seem to have been established until the middle of the fourteenth century, some forty or fifty years later than that in Coventry, but once in production it rapidly became the most important in the Midlands. It is not entirely clear how the tile makers first came there. It seems possible that they worked at various sites in Derbyshire, particularly at Repton, without setting up a major commercial industry and then moved on to sites in Nottinghamshire. Beauvale Priory, founded in 1343, has yielded the most comprehensive series of patterns. Lenton on the outskirts of Nottingham has yielded traces of several kilns. It might well be that it was from Lenton that tile makers moved into Nottingham itself and allied themselves with the flourishing pottery industry there. Kilns for the manufacture of pottery and tiles have been found in the same area in Nottingham, but no tile kiln has been published. White-firing clay for the inlay was available locally here as in Coventry, but it is interesting to notice that in both places this was used increasingly sparingly. Nottingham tiles were distributed over Nottinghamshire, Derbyshire, Leicestershire and parts of Yorkshire, and there may have been a link with the Warwickshire industry.

A selection of tiles of this type is illustrated on Plate VII. All of these patterns are known from other sites as well as those from which the tiles are illustrated, including places in or near Nottingham itself.

PRINTED TILES OF THE CHILTERN FACTORIES

Another decorated tile industry, roughly contemporary with the Nottingham industry, became established commercially in the

Chilterns in the middle decades of the fourteenth century. Its success may have been due in part to the presence of particularly suitable brick clays, but it was due also to technical developments and commercial organisation. The earliest products of the area employ a shallow inlay of white clay for the decoration, very similar to that used on the Warwickshire and Nottingham tiles of the period, but at Penn in Buckinghamshire this was superseded by another method of applying the decoration, which, for want of a better term, is called printing. This was first noted by Loyd Haberly, who published a book on the tiles of the Oxford region in 1937. He was the first writer to pay serious attention to the technical aspects of the craft. He postulated that the Penn tiles were decorated, not by first stamping the design on the tiles and then filling the depressions with white clay, but by a method which combined both processes, namely by stamping the tile with a die dipped in white slip and thus printing the design on the surface. Such a method would reduce the amount of white clay used on each tile and the labour involved in applying it. He carried out a number of practical experiments, to which he refers in his book on the Oxfordshire tiles, but unfortunately he did not publish any detailed record of his results.

Many of the tiles of this region exhibit defects in the application of the design to the tile, such as a smudging of the outlines or incomplete covering of the red clay by the white within the area of the stamped design, that could best be explained by a printing technique. By whatever method it was applied, the layer of white clay is very thin, and the amount of it used is reduced to a minimum. Further economies were practised by the Penn tile makers. They reduced the surface area of each tile to an average of about $4\frac{1}{2}$ inches which enabled them to reduce the thickness to a little under $\frac{3}{4}$ inch without the danger that the tile would warp in the kiln. This overall reduction in the size of the tile quarries meant that more of them could be made from a given quantity of clay, they were lighter and easier to handle, a greater number could be stacked in the oven at one firing and loaded into one cart or boat, in fact they could be manufactured and transported more economically than the earlier larger inlaid tiles. One may safely assume that they could be sold at competitive prices, and that the cost of transport, which was not included in the purchase price, could be offset against a lower initial cost per thousand tiles at the kiln.

The Chiltern tilers captured the trade, not only of the surrounding district, but of the whole of the Thames basin below Oxford to London and beyond. This is apparent from the distribution of the tiles, and fortunately some documentary material also survives. This was published by Christopher Hohler in 1942 in a paper on the medieval paving tiles in Buckinghamshire. It includes records of purchases of tiles from Chiltern tileries. Penn is that most frequently mentioned, but Chalfont, Hedsor and Hedgerly are also recorded. Hedsor may not have had a tilery, but it was probably the place of transfer of the tiles from carriage by cart to boat. The records of purchases cited are spread over the period 1344 to 1358. Most of them refer to roofing tiles, but some paving tiles are also specified mainly in the 1350's. One may perhaps assume that the manufacture of roofing tiles was the primary industry. It is worth mentioning that at this period, and for at least a century before, many roof tiles were given an apron of lead glaze on the lower part of the upper surface, the part that was exposed when they were in position on a roof. The makers of such roof tiles were therefore familiar with the manufacture of lead glazes and the firing of glazed wares. The manufacture of undecorated glazed floor tiles should therefore not have presented them with many new problems and it was only the decorated tiles which required an additional raw material, the white-firing clay, and a new skill in applying it as a decoration.

One paviour was already working at Penn as early as 1332. In a tax roll for Taplow and Penn for that year three men were assessed on the stocks of tiles and lime that they held. They are named as: Henry Tyler, Symon the pavyer, and John the tyler. Out of twenty-one persons taxable in the two places they are the only ones to be assessed on anything besides grain and livestock. The total of the tax payable by these three tilers, 6s. 4¼d., was almost as high as the total of 6s. 10¼d. payable jointly by the lord of the manor and his mother for the manor of Penn. This is an interesting indication of the prosperity of the industry at a date before it can be considered to have reached its peak. Henry Tyler's stock was valued at 10⅔ pence per thousand tiles. These were probably roof tiles. The stocks of Symon the pavyer and John the tyler were both valued at 2s. per thousand tiles, and these may be assumed to have been floor tiles but whether decorated or plain there is no means of finding out. The records of sales are for the period after the Black Death when prices had risen. Roof tiles then seem to have been sold at from 2s. to 3s. 6d. per thousand, possibly depending upon whether they were glazed or unglazed, and floor tiles at prices ranging from 6s. to 8s. per thousand, perhaps depending upon the proportion of them that were decorated.

It is not known how long the industry continued to flourish. In 1368 the vicar of Penn was murdered by his servant and in the subsequent enquiry, one of the vicar's four nearest neighbours, who stood as surety for each other, is named as John Paviere, perhaps a son of Symon the pavyer or of John the tyler mentioned in 1332. A William Pavyer is recorded as a member of a jury in 1479. By that time the name may no longer indicate the man's trade, but it could still do so. A tyle house at Tyler Ende, Penn, is referred to in a lease in 1512 and this suggests that tile making was still in progress there in the early sixteenth century. It is generally supposed that the manufacture of decorated floor tiles at Penn died out before the end of the fourteenth century. It is probable that this more specialised industry was grafted on to an already well established general tile making industry in the second quarter of the fourteenth century, and that it persisted for two or perhaps three generations and was then given up, leaving the local general tile industry to carry on as before.

Technically the Penn tiles are good, sound products, well mixed and well fired, and free from flaws and warping. The glaze is rather yellow, fairly uniform and fully vitrified. The designs are adequate but of no artistic merit. Many of them are derivatives of Wessex patterns, mainly of the Chertsey-Westminster group, but at several removes from the originals. These may have come into the area through a Wessex group at Notley Abbey. Plate VIII : 1 shows a tile derived from the Westminster type of hunting scene, and the lion passant on Plate VIII : 3 is based on Wessex proto-types. The one member of a 4-tile pattern illustrated on Plate VIII : 4 uses the same basic shape as the Hailes Abbey tile shown on Plate IV : 4 and the lion's mask is derived from more elaborate renderings used at Chertsey. The heraldic and pseudo-heraldic shields of arms so common in the Midlands in the fourteenth century are virtually absent from the Chiltern repertory of patterns. Plate VIII : 2 shows one of the few examples recorded.

A large number of the Penn designs, more than half of those listed by Hohler in Buckinghamshire, are repeating patterns, and in most of these the basic decorative element is a circle or a circular band. The unit is either one tile or a set of four identical tiles. In the four-tile unit one quarter of the basic circular motif appears on each tile. Figure 2 illustrates an example of this. It will

Fig. 2. A repeating four-tile pattern based on a single component decorated with one quarter of each of two contiguous circular patterns. From the fourteenth-century factory site at Penn, Buckinghamshire. Drawn by Miss M. O. Miller.

be noticed that the repeating element is introduced by the quarter of a subsidiary circular motif in the outer corners of the tiles. Patterns of this type, though usually without the repeating element in the corners, are fairly common in other districts. The repeating design of circles based on the unit of a single tile may well have been evolved at Penn. Plate VIII : 5 is an example of this type of pattern. On any one tile the central motif is an octofoil flanked by four quarter circles, but when a number of these tiles are laid together the main motif is a series of contiguous circles containing

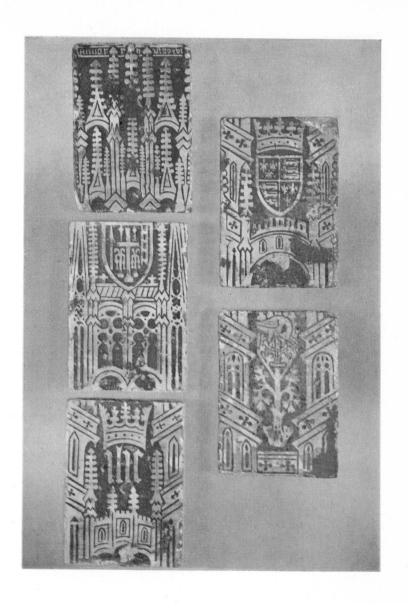

C. Five tiles from the Priory Church, Great Malvern, Worcestershire, forming a section of wall panel bearing the date 36 Henry
VI (1457-8). General Collection.

D. Sixteen tiles forming one complete pattern from a pavement from Canynges House, Bristol. Rutland Collection, Canynges pavement.

lions' masks and fleurs de lys, with the subsidiary motif of an octofoil in the spaces between the circles. This method of arranging the elements of the design in relation to the single tile is rare elsewhere except on later tiles derived from the Penn series such as that illustrated on Plate IX : 1.

It is interesting to notice that in their heyday the Penn tilers were supplying these standardised mass produced tiles, not only to the little parish churches of the neighbourhood which had not been able to afford tiled floors before, but also to the great royal establishments such as Westminster Palace and Windsor Castle and to the Abbeys at Westminster and Chertsey where less than a century before the thirteenth-century craftsmen were producing their masterpieces. Then, as now, the availability of mass produced goods acted as a great leveller.

LATER PRINTED TILES

A modified form of the Chiltern printing technique seems to have been adopted in other areas. Whereas on the Chiltern tiles the white design is flush with the surface of the tiles, on the later printed tiles from other areas the design tends to be depressed below the surface of the tiles. This meant that the very thin white slip was subject to less wear than when it was flush with the surface and to that extent it might be considered to be a technical advance, but in other respects few of the later printed tiles are as well made as the Chiltern products.

In the London area a series of tiles based mainly on Penn designs exhibits this characteristic. They are represented in the collections of the London, Guildhall and British Museums, and have been found at Westminster, Baynard's Castle, Merton Priory and many sites in the City of London often not accurately specified. They probably belong to the late fourteenth and early fifteenth centuries, and their distribution suggests that they were manufactured in or near to London. It is possible that tilers from Penn moved to London and established a factory where there was a ready market for their goods and no need for an elaborate organisation of transport and that the Penn industry ceased to manufacture decorated tiles when the London industry began to do so. A pair of tiles from Westminster is illustrated on

Plate IX : 2. The design is very close to a Penn design, but the tiles themselves are inferior: they are thin, slightly warped, and a large stone has erupted in the surface of one of them. The designs are unevenly printed, parts being missed altogether.

Other supposedly later series are also recognisable in London and the south east. One series occurring in East Kent with outliers in London includes designs based on Wessex types not represented in the Chiltern group. This industry is thought to have been centred at Tyler Hill, Canterbury. The six tiles illustrated on Plate IX : 1 are from East Kent. This repeating pattern has affinities with the Penn pattern illustrated on Plate VIII : 5. Plate IX : 4 shows one tile with a similar type of pattern from Baynard's Castle, London. There are several other groups of tiles which have not yet been linked with a particular place of manufacture. All are of poor quality. In the worst the body clays are badly mixed, the designs are deeply and unevenly depressed below the surface, the surfaces are not flat and the edges are not straight, in fact it is surprising that anyone was willing to buy them. The two mounted knights, Plate IX : 5, from the site of Holy Trinity Priory, Aldgate, London and Plate IX : 3 of unknown provenance but identical with fragments found on the site of Merton Priory, both illustrate these degenerate features.

A completely different series of printed tiles has been recognised in the Midlands in the fifteenth century. These were first discussed by Miss Whitcomb in her catalogue of Leicestershire tiles published in 1956. These seem to have been centred on Coventry and to belong in the main to the latter half of the fifteenth century. The repertory of designs is different from those of the fourteenth-century Chiltern series or the various fifteenth-century series in London and the south east. They continue the earlier Midland traditions of heraldic and pseudo-heraldic motifs and large composite designs employing decorated circular bands and a lot of crude naturalistic foliage.

THE MALVERN SCHOOL

Apparently at the same time as the printed tile industry was being established in the Warwickshire area a revival of the manufacture of inlaid tiles was taking place in the Severn basin, an area apparently unaffected by the mass produced printed tiles of the fourteenth and fifteenth centuries and one in which the Wessex tradition may have lingered on. The tiles are well made, larger and thicker than most of the printed tiles, and the decoration is neatly executed in a shallow inlay, rarely deeper than $\frac{1}{16}$ inch and often much shallower. The designs are well drawn and elaborate and occupy an unusually large proportion of the surface. Many are too intricate to be individually effective in a floor but they were combined in larger overall patterns which took into account the architectural features with which they were associated to form a very splendid whole.

The tile makers were successful in reproducing small and legible inscriptions and most fortunately at Gloucester and Great Malvern these include dates. Abbot Sebroke's pavement before the high altar in Gloucester cathedral includes the date 1455, and the tile wall panels which surrounded the high altar in the priory church at Great Malvern included two dates: A.D. 1453, and 36 Henry VI which was 1457-8. The British Museum possesses one complete panel from the upper row at Great Malvern. The tiles forming this are illustrated on Colour Plate C.

It is clear that the paving works at both places were in progress at the same time, and some patterns were used at both. In the nineteenth century remains of a tile kiln were found near the priory church at Great Malvern. It is stated that the tiles found in it were of the type found in the priory church. Another kiln for the manufacture of tiles of this type was found at St Mary Witton, near Droitwich, but no record of the exact designs associated with it was published.

Tiles of this type are known for convenience as the Malvern School. It is very unlikely that there was a factory at Great Malvern which supplied more than the local area. The tiles are distributed widely through the Severn basin and along the coast of South Wales as far as St David's, but although the repertory of designs is fairly constant, they are reproduced with minor variations of size and motif, and in slightly different fabrics. For example the sanctuary at St David's cathedral still retains a fine pavement which closely resembles Abbot Sebroke's pavement at Gloucester, but all the tiles at St David's are smaller and could not have been stamped with the same blocks. It seems very probable that the Malvern school tilers were organised in the same way as their earlier Wessex counterparts, in bands of travelling craftsmen who set up their kilns in the places where the tiles were required. On the other hand they did sell their tiles commercially. The museum possesses a complete and very fine pavement from the house of William Canynges, a leading Bristol merchant. This pavement contains most of the designs used in St David's cathedral and a number of others, some associated with Heytesbury. None of them has any connection with Canynges himself, and the tiles are either remainders from other special orders or repeats of designs made for other customers.

The pavement is composed of the great sixteen-tile patterns characteristic of the Malvern school, alternating with four-tile patterns within a border of plain dark tiles, all set diagonally to the axis of the room. One of the sixteen-tile patterns is illustrated on Colour Plate D.

Malvern school tiles are also distributed up the Severn valley into Shropshire, and up the Warwickshire Avon at least as far as Stratford. A kiln manufacturing Malvern school tiles was found in the group of kilns already mentioned at Lenton. This was a great surprise as only one tile of this type was known in the area, significantly this was from Lenton. All of the tiles found with this kiln were waste through opaque glaze and no pattern could be seen until the glaze had been chipped off. It is possible that this disaster ruined the band of craftsmen who had set up the kiln. The presence of Malvern school tilers at Lenton, so far from the original centre of manufacture, demonstrates that in the last phase the craftsmen were certainly itinerant.

LATE FIFTEENTH-CENTURY AND SIXTEENTH-CENTURY
TILES

In Warwickshire the Malvern designs were taken over and modified, probably by local craftsmen. Degenerate versions occur at various sites in Coventry and at Stoneleigh Abbey and Wormleighton. These continued to be repeated in ever degenerating forms and occur in Leicestershire and Buckinghamshire also. In Buckinghamshire the site of a kiln manufacturing tiles of the latest known derived type was found at Little Brickhill and some of the material from it is in the British Museum. Christopher Hohler, in his paper on Buckinghamshire tiles already mentioned, cites records of payments for roofing tiles from Brickhill in 1527 and 1530. It is not known whether the decorated paving tiles were being manufactured as late as this, but a date in the first quarter of the sixteenth century is probable. Plate x : 1 shows four tiles of a repeating pattern of this type from the site of Dunstable Priory. These demonstrate the tendency of these designs to appear as angular outline drawings in the red body clay with the rest of the surface covered in the white slip.

If decorated tiles as poor in quality as the Little Brickhill series were all that the industry of the period was capable of producing it might have been expected to die out, but in fact some excellent inlaid tiles of the same period survive from Hailes Abbey in Gloucestershire. These were specially designed for Anthony Melton, Abbot of Hailes from 1509 to 1527. The designs include his name, Plate x: 2, various monograms of his initials and punning rebuses including a barrel or tun for Melton and the crosier and mitre of his office. Other designs include some well-drawn birds, Plate x : 3, and a fleur de lys counterchanged on the axis of the centre petal. Technically and artistically these are beautiful tiles.

Another group of inlaid tiles found in excavations at Blackfriars, Gloucester, includes heraldic designs which show that they were specially commissioned for Llanthony Priory, Gloucester, in the middle of the sixteenth century. These are directly inspired by tiles of the Malvern school and are in no way degenerate. It is also possible that some inlaid tiles in the West Country were made at an even later date. Nevertheless, the main impetus of the inlaid tile industry was spent before the middle of the sixteenth century.

Relief Tiles

EARLY RELIEF TILES

During the whole of the period in which the two-colour inlaid and printed tiles enjoyed such wide popularity, tiles decorated by other methods continued to be made. Particularly in eastern districts north of the Thames, served by ports trading with the Rhineland, tiles decorated in relief were popular. The pattern was either in raised relief or depressed counter-relief, the former being commoner. Each tile was a single colour, glazed yellow or dark green, or less frequently, light green or brown. This type of decoration is known on the Continent from Switzerland to Friesland. It is possible that some of the relief tiles found in England were imported but it is probable that most of them were made here.

A thirteenth-century kiln at North Berwick in Scotland is apparently the earliest of the few kilns known to have manufactured tiles decorated in relief. It supplied the convent there with some beautiful tiles on which well-drawn designs are raised in high rounded relief. The discovery on the kiln site of an unglazed waster suggests that some of these tiles were biscuit fired, a continental, not an English, technique, and it seems possible that some continental craftsmen went to North Berwick specially to do the job, but it should be noted that the waster from North Berwick in the British Museum, illustrated on Plate XI : 1, was definitely glazed before it was fired, the usual English practice.

The most important sites in England from which relief tiles of thirteenth-century date have been found are the monasteries of Swineshead, Repton, Revesby, St Albans and Butley. The designs and techniques used at Butley Priory in Suffolk bear the closest resemblance to those from North Berwick. They are not identical but they could be by the same hand. The tiles from Repton in Derbyshire were made in a kiln found on the site in the nineteenth century, and those tiles from Revesby in Lincolnshire, which are identical with them, were probably made there too. The relief, though less bold than at North Berwick, is high and well rounded. An example is shown on Plate XI : 3. The tiles from Swineshead in Lincolnshire are unknown elsewhere, and, if one may judge by the style of decorative pattern, probably slightly later in date than the rest of this early group of large, thick tiles, decorated in high relief.

St Alban's Abbey and its dependencies have supplied the greatest variety of designs. The majority of them were probably made in the earlier half of the thirteenth century at or near the abbey, but unfortunately no kiln has been found. The presbytery of the Abbey church is paved with nineteenth-century replicas of the thirteenth-century tiles. One of the originals is shown on Plate XI : 7. St Albans also has a number of other apparently early tiles decorated in uncommon techniques, some being stamped and unglazed, others having polychrome glazes.

From Dale Abbey in Derbyshire come some very large, clumsy, green glazed tiles, decorated with stamped patterns in counter relief. The stamps are much smaller than the tiles and are combined in various ways. The results are crude and it is difficult to assign a date. They have the appearance of an early experiment. One, decorated with two mounted knights and some badly placed fleurs de lys, is illustrated on Plate XI : 2.

THE FACTORY AT BAWSEY

The latter half of the fourteenth century saw the establishment of a flourishing relief tile industry in East Anglia comparable with the Chiltern printed tile industry centred on Penn. The factory site was at Bawsey near King's Lynn, and local tradition maintained that it belonged to the monks of Castle Acre. There is no documentary evidence for this, but large numbers of tiles from this kiln have been found at Castle Acre, including some bearing shields of arms appropriate to the Priory, such as that illustrated on Plate XII : 2. The wide distribution of these tiles in the hinterland of the Wash suggests that whoever owned the kilns enjoyed a period of considerable prosperity.

One tile in the Bawsey series can be given a date. This has an inscription asking for prayer for the soul of Nicholas de Stowe, who was vicar of Snettisham. His will was proved in Norwich in 1376. The example illustrated on Plate XII : 1 came from the kiln site.

The Bawsey tiles, like their Chiltern counterparts, are small and thin, averaging just under four inches square and three quarters of an inch thick. Thus the minimum amount of clay was used and the weight of the tiles was kept low for ease in handling and economy in transport. The designs are not exciting, but the earlier ones are competent and the curvilinear pattern illustrated on Plate XII: 3 shows that the original block cutter could handle his medium. The same cannot be said of later blocks, cut to replace those that wore out. These tend to be angular and heraldic designs are not correctly reproduced. This is illustrated by the three versions of the arms of England illustrated on Plate xii 4, 5 and 6, 5 being the most degenerate. Some of the designs are in relief, some in counter-relief. Some, such as the arms of England already mentioned, exist in both forms. Whether the design is raised or sunk, the relief is flat at the top and bottom and shows very little attempt at internal detail except on the animals and birds and on these the results are rather crude.

The glazes are dark green and yellow over a light slip. A large proportion of the tiles dug from the waste heaps at the kiln site had been rejected because of failure to fuse the glaze, but this was probably an error of firing and on the perfect examples the glazes are good. In spite of their artistic limitations the tiles from Bawsey made an effective pavement, arranged, as they were for example at Castle Acre, in groups of four surrounded by plain glazed quarries of contrasting colour.

Although the waste heaps at Bawsey have been dug and the British Museum possesses a large number of tiles from them, it seems improbable that the remains of the kilns themselves have been located. They have certainly not been recorded.

LATER RELIEF TILES

There are sporadic occurrences of other types of tile decorated in relief dating from the fourteenth century, mainly in East Anglia. Occasionally a tile was stamped with a pattern that was normally inlaid in white but the inlay was omitted and a single colour tile decorated in counter-relief resulted. This seems to have happened in most areas at one time or another, and may be regarded as accidental. There is, however, a fairly late but not securely dated series in the Midlands in which the designs are derived from two colour examples but the white clay was intentionally omitted. At Maxstoke in Warwickshire, tiles decorated with the same stamp have been found both with and without the white clay.

The biggest group of tiles of this type found so far, comes from the site of a leper hospital at Burton Lazars in Leicestershire. A piece of pavement was found *in situ* in the chancel, and this and a number of other tiles from the site are now in the British Museum. These include thirteen designs in relief, of which ten were recorded in Melton Mowbray church in the nineteenth century. The designs, most of which are heraldic, appear to be derived from Maxstoke and other late Warwickshire patterns. The example illustrated on Plate xi : 4 is nearly identical with one from Maxstoke, but that on Plate xi : 5 looks like the prototype of a Little Brickhill pattern. A date towards the end of the fifteenth century or early in the sixteenth century therefore seems the most probable for the Burton Lazars series.

Technically the Burton Lazars tiles are very bad and if the piece of pavement had not been found *in situ* one would have thought that they were wasters. Many are warped and the glaze is rarely properly vitrified. As the latest known products of the medieval relief tile industry they are as dreary as are the Little Brickhill tiles for the inlaid and printed groups.

One later group of relief tiles is known. These tiles are of medieval type but not of medieval date. They come from Devon where tiles of lead glazed grey earthenware, decorated in high, rounded relief, continued to be made as an anachronistic survival into the eighteenth century. One of these from the site of North Walk pottery Barnstaple, bearing the initials T W and the date 1708, is shown on Plate xi : 6. Another design incorporated the date 1655. It is interesting to notice that not only are fabric and technique medieval but the design, a fleur de lys, is one of the commonest medieval decorative motifs.

LINE IMPRESSED TILES

Linear designs stamped on to single coloured mosaic tiles have already been mentioned and an example from the site of Pipewell Abbey, Northamptonshire, is illustrated on Plate 1 : 3. The designs associated with mosaic were usually small rosettes of various forms. The technique of decorating with impressed linear designs was more widely used on rectangular tiles without any mosaic element. Both types have been found at Coggeshall in Essex, and the British Museum possesses a number of the rectangular type from St Albans Abbey. The most elaborate surviving pavement which contains tiles decorated in this technique is in Prior Crauden's

Chapel at Ely. This is an elaborate pavement with inlaid mosaic, and line impressed elements and as the central panel before the altar it has a representation of Adam and Eve line incised by hand. Remains of a similar pavement are said to have existed at Higham Ferrers, Northamptonshire, in the last century. A number of tiles of a related line impressed series have been recovered from the site of Pipewell Abbey, Northamptonshire, and are now in the British Museum. These contain representations of animals, grotesques and human figures, all well drawn. One of these is illustrated on Plate 1 : 5. Some of the designs look as if they might have been incised by hand, but the fact that when more than one example of a pattern survives the lines are identical, demonstrates that these were mechanically reproduced.

Each tile was a single colour, either a bright yellow or green. Prior Crauden's Chapel was built about 1324–5 and the pavement is contemporary with the building. It seems probable that all of the tiles decorated in this technique, found in East Anglia and the East Midlands were made at about this date.

Also of earlier fourteenth-century date, and probably related to this line-impressed group, is a frieze of wall tiles found in or near Tring in Hertfordshire, and decorated with pictures of episodes taken from apocryphal stories about the childhood of Christ. The technique is more elaborate because, after the pictures had been incised on a slip coated tile, the slip was removed from the background so that the finished tiles have raised yellow pictures on a brown ground. The figure drawing is superior to any at Ely or Pipewell and these rank as masterpieces among medieval decorated tiles. Eight of them are in the British Museum and two in the Victoria and Albert Museum. One example depicting Christ as a child at school is illustrated on Plate xiv.

An entirely different group of line impressed designs occurs in the North-West Midlands with parallels in and around Dublin. The patterns do not include human figures but consist mainly of geometric shapes, squares, circles, quatrefoils and vesicas, combined with oak or vine leaves. The manufacture of this series may have begun at Repton, Derbyshire, where some were found in association with a kiln. An example from Beauchief Abbey, Derbyshire, is illustrated on Plate 1 : 4. This group may date from the latter part of the fourteenth century.

Probably related to these, but cruder and containing elements of counter relief, is a series found mainly in Staffordshire and Shropshire. These tiles were probably made in the fifteenth century but no examples have yet been found in a closely dated context or associated with a kiln or a heap of wasters. On the basis of distribution, Stafford, or another site in North Staffordshire, seems the most likely place of manufacture. There tend to be a number of variants of the basic designs, a characteristic which is noticeable among the poor quality fifteenth-century tiles of the London area also. Two tiles, one from Nantwich church, Cheshire, and the other from St Giles' church, Newcastle-under-Lyme, Staffordshire, are shown on Plate 1 : 6 and 7. No less than eight variants of this design have been recorded from Stafford itself.

Conclusion

It is not possible within the scope of this booklet to cover all the details of the decorated floor tile industry in medieval England. The main branches have been outlined. It is known that other craftsmen and other factories produced decorated tiles. The later fourteenth and earlier fifteenth centuries seem to have been the period when mass production of factory produced tiles was at its peak, and as is to be expected, minor local production seems to have been most frequent at the times when mass produced tiles were not available. Many of these local products are of inferior quality and off the main stream of development.

Throughout the period, the use of decorated floor tiles in any quantity was confined to the lowland zone of England. There, however, they became so common that after the middle of the fourteenth century few buildings of any standing were without them. Their survival in monastic buildings is due to the fact that the monasteries were dissolved just at the period when these tiles went out of fashion; in domestic buildings they were replaced by other floors more in accordance with sixteenth-century taste.

At the time that the monasteries were dissolved the parish churches entered a period during which interest centred on furnishing rather than structure, and many had a minimum amount of structural alteration until the latter part of the nineteenth century. By that time the surviving medieval tiles were noted and frequently preserved, though generally not *in situ*. The increasing interest in the excavation of late medieval secular buildings has led to the discovery of tiles in such buildings identical with those found in the ecclesiastical buildings of the neighbourhood.

The location of the factory industries doubtless depended in part upon the availability of raw materials and the means of distributing the finished products and in part upon the presence of competent craftsmen and of persons able and willing to finance and organise the enterprise. Our information about the fascinating problem of who was responsible for the manufacture of decorated tiles in this country is still unfortunately scanty, but it is now certain that the theory that the entire industry was carried out by the monastic houses is an over simplification of the facts.

Bibliography

There is no comprehensive standard work on English medieval tiles. A few general surveys were published in the nineteenth century. A large number of articles on more limited aspects of the subject are contained in national and local archaeological and antiquarian periodicals from the middle of the nineteenth century onwards. A selection of the most useful books and papers is listed below.

GENERAL

NICHOLS, JOHN GOUGH, *Examples of Decorative Tiles, sometimes termed encaustic*, London, 1845.

RENAUD, FRANK, 'The Uses and Teachings of Ancient Encaustic Tiles', *Transactions of the Lancashire and Cheshire Antiquarian Society*, Vol. IX, Manchester, 1892.

SHAW, HENRY, *Specimens of Tile Pavements*, London, 1858.

WARD PERKINS, J. B., 'English Medieval Embossed Tiles', *Archaeological Journal*, Vol. XCIV, 1938.

CATALOGUES

HOBSON, R. L., *Catalogue of the Collection of English Pottery in the Department of British and Mediæval Antiquities . . . of the British Museum*, London, 1903, pp. 1–51.

LANE, ARTHUR, *A Guide to the Collection of Tiles*, Victoria and Albert Museum, London, 1939, 2nd edition 1960, chapters III and IV.

WARD PERKINS, J. B., *London Museum Catalogues, No. 7. Medieval Catalogue*. London, 1940, pp. 230–253.

REGIONAL

CHATWIN, PHILIP B., 'The Medieval Patterned Tiles of Warwickshire', *Transactions of the Birmingham Archaeological Society*, Vol. LX (1936) published 1940.

EAMES, ELIZABETH, 'The Products of a Medieval Tile Kiln at Bawsey, King's Lynn, *Antiquaries Journal*, Vol. XXXV, 1955.
'The Canynges Pavement', *Journal of the British Archaeological Association*, Vol. XIV, 1951.
'A Tile Pavement from the Queen's Chamber, Clarendon Palace, dated 1250–2', *ibid.*, Vols. XX, XXI, 1957–8.
'A Thirteenth-century tiled Pavement from the King's Chapel, Clarendon Palace', *ibid.*, Vol. XXVI, 1963.

GREENFIELD, B. W., 'Encaustic Tiles of the Middle Ages found in the South of Hampshire', *Proceedings of the Hampshire Field Club*, Vol. II, Part II, 1892.

HABERLY, LOYD, *Mediæval English Pavingtiles*, Oxford, 1937.

HOHLER, CHRISTOPHER, 'Medieval Pavingtiles in Buckinghamshire', *Records of Buckinghamshire*, Vol. XIV, 1942.

KEEN, Laurence, 'A Series of 17th- and 18th-century lead-glazed relief tiles from North Devon', *Journal of the British Archaeological Association*, Vol. XXXII, forthcoming 1969.

KNAPP, G. E. C. 'The Mediæval Paving Tiles of the Alton area of N.E. Hampshire', *Proceedings of the Hampshire Field Club and Archaeological Society*, Vol. XVIII, 1954.
'The Mediæval Tiles of Winchester Cathedral', *Winchester Cathedral Record*, No. 25, 1956.

PARKER, ALFRED, 'Nottingham Pottery', *Thoroton Society Transactions*, Vol. 36, 1932.

PONSONBY, LORD, 'Monastic Paving Tiles ... Shulbrede Priory, Lynchmere', *Sussex Archaeological Collections*, Vol. LXXV, 1934.

STEVENS, FRANK, 'The Inlaid Paving Tiles of Wilts', *Wiltshire Archaeological and Natural History Magazine*, Vol. xlvii, 1935.

WARD, JOHN, 'Notes on the Mediæval Pavement and Wall Tiles of Derbyshire', *Derbyshire Archaeological and Natural History Society Journal*, Vol. 14, 1892.

WHITCOMB, NORMA, *The Medieval Floor-Tiles of Leicestershire*, Leicestershire Archaeological and Historical Society, Leicester, 1956.

KILNS

EAMES, ELIZABETH, 'A Thirteenth-century Tile Kiln Site at North Grange, Meaux, Beverley, Yorkshire', *Medieval Archaeology*, Vol. V, 1961.

GARDNER, J. S. and EAMES, ELIZABETH, 'A Tile Kiln at Chertsey Abbey', *Journal of the British Archaeological Association*, Vol. XVII, 1954.

RICHARDSON, J. S., 'A Thirteenth-century Tile Kiln at North Berwick, East Lothian . . . ', *Proceedings of the Society of Antiquaries of Scotland*, Vol. LXIII, 1928–9.

VIDLER, LEOPOLD A., 'Floor Tiles and Kilns near the site of St. Bartholomew's Hospital, Rye', *Sussex Archaeological Collections*, Vol. LXXIII.

I Counter-relief and line-impressed tiles. 13th-15th centuries.
[Scale 2:5]

II Paving of plain and inlaid tiles. King's Chapel, Clarendon
Palace. Circa 1244. [Scale 1 : 12]

III Drawing of 13th-century inlaid tile mosaic from Chertsey Abbey, Surrey. Published by Henry Shaw. 1858. [Scale 1 : 4]

IV Inlaid tiles. Chertsey-Westminster type. 13th century. [Scale 1:4]

V Paving of plain and inlaid tiles. Queen's Chamber, Clarendon
Palace. 1250–52. [Scale 1 : 10]

VI Inlaid tiles. Wessex school. 13th–14th century. [Scale 3 : 10]

VII Inlaid tiles. Nottingham school. 14th century. [Scale 3 : 10]

VIII Printed tiles. Chiltern factories. 14th century. [Scale 3 : 8]

IX Printed tiles. South-eastern factories. Probably 15th century.
[Scale 1: 3]

X Printed and inlaid tiles. 16th century. [Scale 1 : 4]

XI Relief tiles. 13th–16th centuries. [Scale 1:4]

XII Relief tiles. Bawsey factory. 14th century. [Scale 4 : 10]

SKETCH OF FLOOR
TILING AT STEP A.

←STEP A

XIII Plan of tile mosaic pavement. Byland Abbey. 13th century.

XIV Pictorial tile decorated in sgraffiato. 14th century. [Scale 4 : 7]

XV Substructure of tile kiln *in situ*. Clarendon Palace. Probably
1237–1244.

XVI Model of tile kiln from Clarendon Palace shown on plate XV.

Réseau de bibliothèques Université d'Ottawa Échéance	Library Network University of Ottawa Date Due